I0620194

THE LITTLE GIRL LOOKING BACK AT ME

By

Christena Rollins

Copyright © 2024 Christena Rollins.

All rights reserved. This book or any portion of this book may not be reproduced, distributed, or transmitted in any form by any means including photocopying, recording, or other electronic mechanical methods without the express written permission of the publisher, except in the pace of brief quotations embodied in critical reviews and certain other noncommercial uses permitted by copyright law.

TABLE OF CONTENTS

DEDICATION

This book is dedicated to every young girl and woman who has ever questioned or doubted her importance, every woman who has ever looked in the mirror and saw anything other than a perfect masterpiece created by God, looking back at her.

SPECIAL THANKS!!!

I would like to give a special thanks to someone who came into my life and changed me and how I saw myself. You came into my life at a time when I was ready to fold and give in, you sat on the phone with me for six hours, letting me pour out my feelings, and then encouraged me back to life. You believed in me even when I didn't believe in myself and you never judged me, you stood by my side through a dark place in my life, and not once even while in that place did you doubt the God in my life or did you ever not trust the words that God gave me for you. I thank you for single-handedly doing all the paperwork and everything behind the scenes to get the vision that God trusted me with to come to life. I thought that people like you did not exist until God sent you into my life. I am my sister's keeper! I love you and thank you, Tina Marie!

PREFACE

A Mother's Vision:

When we were children, our mothers told us that we were beautiful and smart and that we could do anything and become whatever we wanted in life if we believed in ourselves.

What our mothers forget to tell us is that everyone in life will not agree with or believe what she has said about us, what she said will be tested.

CHAPTER 1

Her

"I do not want to play with her because she is ugly!" I wanted to break down crying because my feelings were hurt and the other kids on the playground were pointing at me and laughing. I pretended that what was said did not matter and I did not want to play with them anyway. I sat by myself and tried not to stare at the kids playing, wishing I were one of them, before I knew it tears were rolling down my cheeks. My mom said I was beautiful, but I guess the kids on the playground did not agree with her. I always remember this comment and so many others like this, throughout my life. I am more than sure that we all have our own version of heartache and pain that we have felt at some point in our lives. Some are a little more often than others. That is the crippling effect that words can have on our lives when we forget or have not been taught who we are and to whom we belong. God said in Genesis 1:31 KJV, "And God saw everything that he had made, and behold, it was very good." As a kid, that scripture meant nothing to us, so it has no deep and lasting effect. As an adult, however, it does, and my personal take on the scripture is that, regardless of how mean and cruel things

6

are said to you or about you, even if they are hurtful, their truth does not matter. The person who created you and knew you while you were just a seed in your mother's womb, says that everything that he made was VERY GOOD!! which includes you and me.

I remember something that my grandmother used to say, I am sure some of you have heard it at some point in your lives as well. It does not matter what you are called, what matters is what you answer to. That is so profound to me because it is so true. If you know who you are, or not for that matter, why worry about what people say or call you? As an adult, I have come to realize that most people who are mean and say cruel things to and about other people are those who have been hurt at some point or are unhappy with themselves, so they want others to feel the pain that they feel inside. "Hurt people hurt people," it is a known fact. Let us test this theory and be honest with ourselves, we will begin to release our own pain by becoming sympathetic to the people who have hurt us in the past, which leads to forgiveness.

Think back to a time in your past when you were in pain because of something someone had done or said to you. What was your interaction with others like? Were you as friendly and kind as you would be when you are not hurting and emotionally unstable? Or were you a little sharper and more impatient because everything got on your nerves, no matter how small it was? I can be honest, so, I will use myself as an example. I know in the past when I was hurting, I've tried to steer clear of others because, for some reason, I am a little more agitated and short with people, even though most times they are not even the reason that I am hurting. For some reason, we do not know how to process our pain and direct our anger or feelings to the people who have hurt us. The next time that you find yourself in a place where you are hurt or upset, I urge you to try something that has truly helped me. The next time someone says something mean or does something to hurt you, instead of allowing the negative energy to affect you, just remember that they themselves are probably hurting and they do not know how to control or direct their pain. This is not to excuse their behavior, but it does help you not to be drawn into their misery and make you feel just as bad as they do. You may even find out that by responding with a kind word instead of a negative reaction, you could change their attitude and disposition and help them in a minor way. I know that it is not easy to ignore someone who is being mean and cruel, but I have learned that we are in control of our own mood, no one can take our joy unless we allow it, by what we receive into our spirit. I know this from experience.

I remember when I was in grade school, my mother had to attend a lot of parent conferences because I wore my feelings on my shoulder as my mother would say. Every time someone said something mean about me, I would get into an argument, or I would get into a fight. I spent most of my teens fussing, fighting, and defending myself as I would tell my mom. I never understood why my mom would say, "You were not defending yourself; you were entertaining ignorance." I used to be really upset with her because I felt she did not have my back, which is what my kids call it today. I felt like she did not understand me or care about how I felt. As I grew older and began to mature in my way of thinking, I began to understand what she meant by, "I was not defending myself, I was entertaining ignorance." For me to say I was defending myself, simply means that there was some truth to what they were saying. If something is not true, there is no need to defend it or even take the time to give it any attention or your energy for that matter. I now realize that the reason I stayed fussing and fighting was because deep down I was insecure about my looks, so anything that someone said that addressed my looks became a fight. I was unhappy with my looks. I was ugly and because I felt that way, what other people said affected me. I am not saying it was true but because I had heard so many people say it, I began to believe it. I looked at other girls and because I did not look like them, I felt that meant I was ugly. When I was growing up, if you were not light-skinned with nice long relaxed hair, you were not considered pretty. I was a dark-skinned girl with short kinky hair and although we lived in a nice middle-class neighborhood, needless to say, I was not in the pretty girl crowd. So, most of my time was spent alone in my room with my books, pretending not to care about not having many friends. My mom always said that it was their loss because I was perfect, but from where I was standing, I was the one losing out. We start building our self-esteem at a very young age and although it shouldn't be, we base our self-worth and value on what other people say and think of us, so by the time we hit adolescence, we are in full swing of what we let other people tell us about ourselves. Once the cycle has begun, it is almost impossible to reverse.

When I was sixteen, I did not like anything about myself. I found something wrong with everything, no matter how much people would say I was beautiful. When I looked in the mirror, I did not see what they saw. I had been programmed for sixteen years to believe that I was ugly, and I believed it and there was nothing anyone could tell me to change my mind. I did not like myself or anything about myself. I spent most of my time wishing I looked like every girl I thought was pretty, I wanted to be anyone but myself. I never thought about the fact that I was smart or the fact that I had good leadership qualities or that I was kind and would give you the shirt off my back. I just wanted to be pretty like all the other pretty girls as I perceived them to be, nothing else mattered. I was so depressed and unhappy with myself in my teens that I went into this dark place and isolated myself from everyone. I started acting out and getting into trouble a lot. My mom did not know what was going on in my mind. I was making too much out of nothing and because of that, I stopped talking to her because to me, being pretty was everything and she did not understand that. I wasted so much time unhappy with who I was not, that I never took the time to figure out who I was and because of that, I spent most of my adult life feeling lost. I was in and out of relationships because the one thing I wanted, I could not find and that was to be happy and a place to feel like I belonged. I got pregnant when I was eighteen and gave birth to my first son when I was nineteen. I was a mother now and, in a relationship, not knowing anything about being a woman, let alone a mother. I had my second son fifteen months after my first son. Now, with my two sons, I was trying to be a mother in a verbally abusive relationship and at the same time looking for some type of sign that God has not forgotten about me. Most of my nights were spent crying myself to sleep because I felt like I was drowning, and no one could help me.

I was twenty-one with two kids, trying to raise them as best I knew how. My partner and I continued to argue and say mean things to one another, it was getting worse every day. It got so bad that we could not stay in the same room with one another, at that point the cheating started. I stayed even though I knew what he was doing because I felt that I could not raise my two kids on my own. I had to put up with what he was doing because I needed him, and he knew that as well. I grew up in a home with two parents, so I wanted the same for my kids. Four kids later, we still do not really like each other, and I was more lost than I have ever been, all while trying to raise four kids. My kids became my best friends and the only people that I spent my time with. At the age of twenty-six, I was tired and could not take any more of the cheating or the verbal abuse, so we split up. It was hard in the beginning, but I survived. I promised myself that I would never again be put in a place where I had to take being abused in any way or mistreated by a man.

I have never really had to stand on my own two feet and take care of myself and my kids on my own, so this was unfamiliar territory to me, I was scared. I could not go home to my mom, that was not an option. So, at this point, it was swim or drown and drowning was not an option. I had babies depending on me to provide for them, I had to get a job and keep it. I had bills to pay now. I had never paid bills before, so, again I made some bad decisions. I wanted to give my kids the things that I never had. In my mind, I felt that if they had nice clothes like all the other kids, they would not be teased, and they could be a part of the crowd as we called it back then. I never wanted my kids to go through what I had to go through as a child. It did not matter what it took, I was going to make sure of that. I did not pay my bills on time, so we had to move because I got so far behind, I couldn't catch up. I ended up moving in with my kids' grandmother, their dad's mom. I was blessed to have someone like her in my life. She helped me and never judged me. She stepped in and guided me. She watched my kids, her grandkids while I worked and never took a dime from me. I got my first check, and she took me to the bank to open a joint bank account and taught me how to save money. I and my kids lived with her for a few months until I had saved enough money to get my own apartment. Once I had enough money for an apartment, she took me apartment hunting and helped me pick out my first apartment. I was able to get my first apartment without any help from a man. I will never forget what she did for my kids and me, she was truly a God-sent., I know that some will say that she was supposed to because she was their grandmother, but truth be told, no one must do anything for you in this life. Through it all, she never once made me feel bad about myself or spoke mean words to me. I know that everyone is not as fortunate to have someone who can or will take the time to help you when you are down and in need. I do know that if you are fortunate enough to find someone to help you when you are struggling and lost, be grateful. Life is full of difficulties, and it is hard enough to navigate through life when you are lost and have no direction like I was. As I sit here writing this with tears-filled eyes, I know that it was only by the grace of God that I have made it this far. For most of my life, I felt alone and did not believe God loved me or could love me because of all the bad choices that I had made in my life. I was so embarrassed that I could not even bring myself to believe that I had a right to talk to God. Now I know that it was not that God would not forgive me or didn't love me, it was me who couldn't forgive myself. I did not believe God loved me because I did not love myself, so how could anyone else? I did not realize that through all the difficulties in my life, it was God who kept me and provided for me. It was God that sent my kid's grandmother into my life to help me, it was God that sent the job, it was God that sent the apartment and it was most definitely God that kept my kids and me covered and safe. When we are going through life, we spend so much time focused on our circumstances, that we are blind to the ways that God is making to bring us out and provide for us. We are never alone. God is always with us no matter where we are, he is there in every situation, and he will always make a way.

Question to Ponder

What hurtful and painful memories from your childhood have you carried into your adulthood?

_____

_____

_____

_____

_____

_____

_____

_____

NOTES

NOTES

NOTES

_____

_____

_____

_____

_____

_____

_____

_____

_____

CHAPTER 2

Need To Belong

We spend our whole life yearning to feel like we belong, to feel special in some way to someone. No one wants to be alone; everyone wants to be loved and feel the closeness of another. Even if that means sacrificing who we really are sometimes. We declare that we will never let someone treat us like dirt or disrespect us, we even tell our friends what they should do about their relationships. We have all the answers for everyone's situation but not our own. Now here we are in a relationship, head over heels in love and he/she feels the way, at least that is what they have told us. In the beginning, everything is perfect, you spend all your time together, you are on cloud nine, and you feel that they are the one.

Two months later, things are beginning to change, phone calls are going unanswered, and you are not spending as much time together because they are too busy. Your gut(intuition) tells you that something is wrong but you ignore it and brush it off because as women we say we want the truth but in actuality, we are really scared of the truth. So, we hide from it as long as we can and make excuses for what is right in our faces. We dance around the truth, the same truth that we pointed out to our friends when they were in the very same situation. It is always easier to see someone else's truth and be blinded to our own.

We know that something is not right but instead of confronting the problem head-on, we try to pretend that it does not exist. Our whole attitude changes and we become this person that suspects everyone no matter who it is. We are in denial, so we do not talk about it to anyone, not even our friends because we don't want anyone to know or to say that we are being stupid. We are now walking around with all these bottled-up emotions and no one to talk to about them, we have become a walking time bomb!

We do not have an outlet for these toxic emotions, so they begin to change us on the inside. We used to be this positive, loving, caring, funny, and full-of-life person. Now we are bitter, angry all the time, and negative because we do not know how to channel our frustration. Now we are mad at the world and everyone in it that shows any sign of happiness because we ourselves are not happy. Our friends do not know who we are anymore, they question us, and we become defensive because we feel that they are tripping. We cannot see ourselves the way they can or the fact that we have changed. We do not want to be embarrassed by a break-up especially after we have bragged about the love of our life and how perfect they were. We pretend that everything is perfect until we are forced to confront what we already have known for a while is going on, a friend, or a friend of a friend witnesses something that now causes you to face the facts. You can no longer hide the truth or pretend that it is not happening. You are forced to deal with the fact that you are being cheated on. For some reason, as women, our initial reaction is to make some excuse for the person who has violated our trust because again, we don't want to admit it to ourselves, and secondly, we don't want to look like fools. Now, we find ourselves making excuses for this person's disrespectful behavior, bad enough that they are cheating. The next person we get angry with is the person who saw them in the first place and said something, we are angry at them because now, they have forced us to acknowledge what we have known all alone.

We confront them by asking questions that we already have the answers to. We know that they are going to lie and deny it and even though we know the truth deep down inside, we want them to lie and say it's not true so that the impact of another failed relationship is not so bad. We blame everyone but the person we need to be blaming and that person is ourselves, if we had dealt with the issue when we first realized there was one, it could have been resolved. But, instead, we pretended it didn't exist, so it got worse and spiraled out of control. We did not confront the problem, so they got sloppy and reckless with our feelings because they felt that there were no consequences for their actions.

We allowed someone to take advantage of us and we were wounded because we did not protect ourselves and our hearts. A person can only do what you allow them to do. We teach people how to treat us by what we are willing to accept, bottom line! Hard truth. If we allow people to mistreat us and disrespect us without confronting and addressing the behavior, then it is our fault that we end up hurt. We all want to be needed and to feel loved, but we cannot sacrifice our dignity and self-respect for something that will not last because it was not built on a foundation of respect, honor, and loyalty. Someone who truly respects you and is loyal to you, would not do something that would bring pain to you. If a person is willing to do something that they know will violate your trust and hurt you, that means that they are selfish and are only concerned about themselves. A selfish person cannot love someone other than themselves and therefore cannot function in a committed and devoted relationship with another person, because they can't truly care for anyone other than the person they see in the mirror. Love is not selfish!

We cannot love and respect ourselves and make it ok for people to do us wrong and accept it. It is human nature that we, as women, are nurturers and we want to be loved, we want to be held and yearn to be needed. We do not like the idea of being alone, so we are willing to accept things that are sometimes toxic to our health, mentally, and emotionally, just to belong.

We get taken advantage of because we are creatures of habit. We want to take care of everyone, it makes us feel important and needed. It gives us purpose. Women have become so accustomed to being cheated on, that somewhere in our being has just accepted it and normalized it, and told ourselves that all men cheat and it's ok to be the other woman/ side chick. Well, I am here to set the record straight, it is not ok to be cheated on and it is most definitely not ok to be the other woman. I heard someone say a few days ago that if we as women do not want our man cheating, we should tell him to keep it in his pants. The statement is true to some extent. Our partners or husbands should not be sleeping with other women outside of the one they are in a relationship with. However, all the responsibility is not solely on the man. We live in a time when men are being honest about the fact that they are married, and women are still engaged in a relationship with these men. I feel that anytime a man is comfortable with saying that he is married, and the other woman is ok with it and gets engaged in a relationship with him, we have a very big problem on our hands. Have we as women completely laid our self-worth down by the wayside? When did we become okay with being anything other than number one and only in a man's life? We say that we want respect but how can we demand respect if we do not value and respect ourselves? To sleep with a man knowing that he is in a relationship is sending the message that it is okay with us that he is lying to both his wife and to us his mistress/side chick/other woman. We are saying that it is okay for him to treat us as if we have no value and that we are insignificant. When a man sleeps with more than one woman at a time, he has no respect for either woman and knowingly allowing him to do so says that we are okay with him disrespecting us. We are important, we are worth so much more than what we allow and accept. We have led ourselves to believe that it is the wife's problem if her husband cheats and that we are somehow special because it is us that he is cheating with. In all actuality, we are no more special than the wife that he is cheating on. If it were not you, it would be someone else, and probably will be in the near future. We must understand that sex is just that to a man. A man can have sex with a woman and have no attachment to her at all and never see her again. Most women are the opposite, if we have sex with you, it is understood that we are now in a relationship, no doubt about it. We as women must understand who we are and who we were created to be. God says in Psalm 139: 14, "We are fearfully and wonderfully made."

We must understand that we are more than just a one-night stand or a fling to some men. We are more than some other woman that a man uses for sex outside of his wife because he is selfish. God honored women with the ability to bring life into the world, without

24

women life would cease to exist, that itself is a very precious gift that God entrusted only to women. We are as special to God as we should be to ourselves. We were created lacking nothing and we should not accept being treated as if we are from no one. We are courageous, smart, beautiful, and nurturing creatures by habit, and we should not be mistreated or taken advantage of because of the loving and caring beings we are. We must start holding men accountable for their actions and understand this, please! A man is not going to stay somewhere that he is not happy. They do not care what the circumstances are, or how many children they have, period. We must stop letting men tell us that they are not happy and that they are planning to leave their wives because at the end of the day, if they were truly going to leave their wives, they would've done so by now. This is just a lie that has worked for so long, and they continue to use it. If we are willing to be honest just for a moment, how many relationships that started from cheating have actually ended in marriage or long-term successful relationships? If a man knows that you are willingly cheating with him knowing that he has a wife. Do you honestly believe that he would trust you to be solely committed to him and not do the same to him if the opportunity presented itself? I do not think so, and vice versa. Would you trust him knowing that he cheated on his wife with you? I do not think so, meaning that this entire fling is a waste of time, and you are not getting anything meaningful out of this relationship. Are you okay with wasting your time and missing Mister Right because you are playing around with someone else's Mister Right? We are allowing men to use our bodies like disposable wipes. Our bodies are precious and sacred and should be treated with the utmost respect. We deserve to be in a relationship with someone who is committed solely to us and loves and respects us and our bodies. It is time for us as women to unite and stand together instead of looking at each other as the enemy. We are not the enemy and there is no reason that we should feel the need to compete with one another.

God created each of us to be different in our own unique way. He did not create any two of us the same, we are supposed to be different. It is time that we embrace our uniqueness. We all have something that only we can offer as an individual. Let us take a stand and come together. We are so much more powerful together than divided. We have the power to change the way that men treat us. We teach people how to treat us by what we allow and accept from people. It is time that we change what society has decided is acceptable by redefining our own identity and our own voice. It is time for virtuous women to rise and take their place. It is time for our voices to be heard. It is time for the world to see who we truly are, powerful, smart, and courageous women who will not accept anything less than being treated as such.

Question to Ponder

What are some of those choices that you have made throughout your life, that when you look back at them now, you know that they were made from a need to belong?

_____

_____

_____

_____

_____

_____

_____

NOTES

NOTES

NOTES

CHAPTER 3

The Comparison

For decades, society has told us what to wear, what to weigh, and how to look and because of this, we live in a time where we are constantly competing with one another for something. We are competing on the job for better positions, for the attention of men, etc. We have let society decide who we are and what we should be and due to this, we feel that we are in constant competition with one another as if we are going to win some type of prize. God says in Galatians 6:4, "But let every man prove his own work, and then shall he have to rejoice in himself alone, and not in another."

What this scripture says to me is not to worry about what someone else has, focus on yourself and be the best that you can be. If you take the time to focus on yourself and what you want to do and be, you will not have time to focus on someone else and what they are doing. Be happy with yourself and get to know who you are and what is important to you. We spend so much time in our lives trying to compete and mimic someone else's life, that we lose ourselves or never really get to find out who we are and become that person. When we place more importance on what someone else thinks of us or what we should be, we will never grow and evolve, life is all about growth. We must get to a place where we are free to be who God created us to be and be alright with it. No two people were created the same, so no matter how hard we try to be like someone other than ourselves, it will never be true because that is not who we are deep down inside. If we let society continue to tell us who we are, we will be forever changing with the times and never be able to genuinely enjoy the process of growth. Society is not consistent enough to listen to them, they are unstable. Today yellow is the color and tomorrow it has changed to blue. God created each of us in our own unique way and no matter how much we may try or want to change that, we will never be completely free or happy until we embrace who we truly are. It takes so much time trying to be like someone else that it becomes frustrating. Get to know yourself by asking questions like, what is your favorite color? What type of foods do you like the most? What are the things that you dislike? Etc. You get where I am going with this. If you find that you cannot answer these basic questions about yourself, then it is time that you start finding the answer to those questions. In the process, you might find that you like the person that you have been running away from and embrace her. We are in control of our own happiness and the only person that can stand in the way of that happiness is you. When we let society tell us who we are, we are allowing them to tell us that we are all the same and no one is unique and that is far from the truth because we are all individuals, and no two people were created the same. We say that slavery was abolished, but has it really?

Slavery is merely nothing but a form of mind control, if you can control someone's mind, then you can tell them what to think, how to dress, etc. So, when we allow society to tell us what is acceptable, how we should dress, and how to wear our hair, we enslave our minds to what they think and therefore we are no longer individuals.

It is time for us to change our way of thinking, it is time for us to decide how we will live and who we will become. It is time for us to free our minds from the things of the world. For some reason, we have been made to believe as women that we need to tear one another down, we need to climb over one another to succeed and once we have succeeded, we need to make sure that no one comes behind us. Well, that is so not true. There is enough room at the top for us all to succeed. We must understand that when we were but a seed in our mother's womb, God knew who we would be because he wrote our lives, we each have our very own destiny and purpose in life. We must understand and know that what God has for us is for us, no one else can fulfill your destiny or complete your purpose but you, because God created you to do it, there is no need to trample over anyone else to get your piece of success because God has already secured your bag. No one can walk in your purpose but you and no one can fulfill your destiny but you. Our blessings are in our purpose, so when we get to know who we are in Jesus, we then begin to walk in our purpose and our blessings are released. If we spend more time finding out what our purpose is, we would not have as much time to focus on someone else's blessings because we would be too busy securing our own blessings. The blessings that God has designed, just for us. We were all created with a purpose and gifts that only we can birth into the world. It is something that only you can do because you were created to do it, no one else can. So, when we truly realize this, we understand that there is no need to feel that we must compete with one another to succeed. We were each born with what we need inside of us to succeed, we all have our own unique purpose designed with us in mind according to our personality, characteristics, and traits.

God said that we are to love our neighbor as we love ourselves. God also said that we are to carry one another's burdens to the throne in prayer. We are supposed to be building one another up and lifting one another, not tearing each other down because of our own insecurities. We were created to be united not divided. The enemy wants to cause division because that is where he operates and controls. We only get one opportunity in life, and I know that I have enough regrets in mine. I do not want to spend one more moment doing something that I will regret later. Time is a precious commodity, and we cannot undo what has already passed and been done. Every day is precious and can only be lived once. So, it is important that we make the most of that day because we can't do it again. If we don't like the way it turned out, then there is nothing we can do because there is no guarantee that there will be a tomorrow, so let's try to make each day count. I always try my best to live by this one rule, 'Treat people the way you want to be treated.' I am not perfect, and I haven't always gotten it right in the past, but I do try my best to get it right daily. Every day should be lived as if there will be no tomorrow.

Question to Ponder

How many times throughout life have you felt like you were pressured into comparing yourself?

_____

_____

_____

_____

_____

_____

_____

NOTES

NOTES

NOTES

CHAPTER 4

She Thinks

When we see a woman who is successful, confident, strong, and comfortable in her own skin, the first thing that comes to some of our minds because of our own insecurities is, "Oh, she thinks she's all that." Why is this phrase so common among women? Why is this the first thing that comes to our minds? We have no clue what this woman has had to go through or what she has lost or the pain that she has had to endure to become the woman that she is today. You cannot get to where she is without going through something similar and that is why she has the confidence that we see in her. She is excited that she was able to make it through all that she has endured. When we are comfortable in our own skin and know that we lack nothing, we can overcome anything because we are strong, smart, and courageous women. We begin to walk in our purpose and become free to move beyond the boundaries that society has placed in our minds. When we are free, we no longer live our lives based on the ideas of what other people think about us, we no longer feel the need to compare ourselves to one another.

God says in Philippians 4:13, "I can do all things through Christ who strengthens me." That scripture says that there is nothing that we cannot do with God on our side. When we truly grasp the meaning of this scripture, we understand that there are no boundaries and that we are limitless to what we can do and achieve through God. When you start to believe in yourself and begin to walk in the power that dwells inside of you, the way you view life and everything around you changes. When we are truly set free, the way we walk, the way we talk, and the way that we see things becomes different. We are no longer concerned with what other people think about us or say about us, we no longer care about the minor details of things like our weight, skin color, etc.

We spend most of our lives living by what society, social media, magazines, television, and the expertise of other people, who have no clue of what's going on in their own lives, let alone tell us what is acceptable. Every day, their opinion changes, so with all this inconsistency, how can we ever discover our true selves if we only heed what the world tells us? We must get to a place where we build a relationship with the one who created us. All the answers that we search for are found in knowing God and he alone will reveal them. In God, we are free to evolve and walk into the fullness of who we were created to be. In God, depression does not exist, low self-esteem no longer exists, and unworthiness is gone. We must reconnect with the little girl inside of us, the little girl who was fearless and had a big imagination. The little girl who was not afraid to dream aloud. She wasn't afraid to fail because she knew that if she got up and tried again, with persistence, she would eventually succeed. She believed she could accomplish anything she set her mind to with determination. When we were little girls, we had a vision for our lives, we knew exactly what we wanted to become and somewhere in the process of growing up, we lost that little girl.

She was brainwashed and led to believe that dreams do not come true. We must go back in time and get familiar with that little girl again. It is time to be reminded of all the things that we have forgotten about ourselves. The little girl looking back at us is waiting for us to become what she dreamed for us, to live the life that she spoke over us. I know that as a little girl, I envisioned so much for my life as little girls do. I was going to be a news reporter, a nurse, or a doctor. I had big dreams for my life. Somewhere along the way, life got a hold of me. beat me down, and made me believe that those things I hoped for were unattainable. In life, things happen that cause us to doubt our ability to achieve the things that we wish for so desperately. Once doubt sets in, we begin to lose hope and before we know it, we settle into our mediocre life and become mad at anyone living the life that we dreamed of. We allow life's setbacks, pain, and heartache to make us bitter. We get angry at the women who have achieved the things that we wanted for ourselves. We are angry because deep down inside, we feel that we have failed ourselves and it is much easier to be angry with someone else than to be angry with the one true person at fault, us. We can do anything and become anything we want to in life with God's strength, discipline, and determination to succeed.

It is never too late to achieve all the things that we dreamed and hoped for as a little girl. We hold the key to our own success. In today's time, no one wants to work for anything. We want it to be handed to us, and we want it to be easy to obtain. If the effort required exceeds our expectations or if the process takes longer than anticipated, we tend to give up if we can't find a quicker route. Everything in life worth having requires sacrifice, nothing comes easy, if it were, everyone would have it. God said in Ecclesiastes 9:11, "The race is not given to the swift, nor the battle to the strong, but to the one who endures to the end."

In life there will be pain, there will be setbacks, and there most definitely will be loss and heartache but we must stay strong and endure to the end. God did not say that everything would be easy, but he did promise never to leave us nor forsake us. We must get back up and know that there is nothing that we can't accomplish with God on our side. God wants us to succeed! The reason that we give up so quickly is because we do not believe in ourselves, deep down inside, we do not believe that we can do it. We allow our thoughts to control us and plant seeds of failure in our minds. Our thoughts tell us things like, you can't do that, you aren't smart enough to do that, you didn't finish school, so you can't get that job, etc. The list goes on. These are just a few examples, but you get the point. We must take control of our thoughts and stop allowing negative thoughts to poison our minds. Our thoughts dictate who we become. If we believe that we can accomplish it, we will. If we believe that we cannot achieve it, then we will not. It is as simple as that. We must start motivating ourselves and speak life over ourselves just like we did as little girls. Everything that we need for survival is in us already; we just have to tap into the power that God has given us. We have to speak about those things that are not as if they are, and persist in doing so until we see change. We must put in the work required to succeed. We've got to stop being lazy and expecting everything to be handed to us at no cost and with no sacrifice. Everything comes at a price (meaning if you want it, you must work for it). You must be willing to put in the work required to reap the benefits of success. Every person who has achieved remarkable success, whether inherited or not, has worked for it, and even if it was inherited, maintaining it requires ongoing effort. Success does not come overnight, it takes discipline and persistence. If you are lacking one of these two values you will not get far. Everyone wants success but not everyone wants to work for it or endure the pain, heartache, and loss that it takes to achieve success. So, the next time you see someone who has achieved success, don't say, "Oh she thinks she is all that," but rather think about all that she must have endured and lost along the way to get to where she is. It is time we move past the fear that cripples us and keeps us standing still and afraid to try because we are afraid to fail. If we never try, we will never know if we can achieve it. I believe trying and failing is better than living with a life of regret and uncertainty because you never tried. We must experience failures throughout life, but the failures strengthen us and bring wisdom. For every failure in life, there is also a lesson attached to it. If we live a life of fear and never attempt to achieve anything then we are not living, we are only existing. If we allow fear to keep us captive, we will never experience life in its fullness. Success comes to those who go out and get it and are not afraid to fail trying. Playing it safe will only keep you stagnant and God did not mean for us to stand still, his word says that he wants us to prosper and the only way to do that is in constant movement. We are all capable of success. The tools needed are in each of us. All we need to do is begin to apply them, the first step is to change the way we view ourselves. Stop letting doubt creep in and tell us that we cannot, and start saying that we can. "We can do all things through Christ who strengthens us."

God did not say we could do some things, he said we could do all things. There are no boundaries in God, so we must stop putting limits on what we can achieve. Stop saying and thinking it cannot be done and just do it, and do not accept failure as an option. You must get tired of just getting by and living from paycheck to paycheck. That is no way to live, especially if you have children depending on you. You must get desperate because then and only then will you decide to make a change. As the saying goes, "When you get sick and tired of being sick, you will take the necessary steps to change your situation." I was tired of standing still and just barely making ends meet. I knew something had to change. I began to ask myself questions and as I began to answer those questions that I asked myself, I realized that I was the only person standing in the way of my success. Nothing in life matters more than what you think of yourself, your thoughts have the power to make or break your future. Once I realized that I was the reason that I had not achieved the things I wanted in life, I began to take steps to change my circumstances.

You must want change; it is not going to knock on your front door. Today, I am working on an advertisement for my hair care line that I created in my kitchen, and I am writing this book right now to help other people like me, in hopes that they will also take the steps toward success. If I could do it, I know that you can as well, you just must believe in yourself. It is time for women to rise.

Question to Ponder

How many times in life have you found yourself making a judgment call of someone simply based on outer appearances?

_____

_____

_____

_____

_____

_____

_____

NOTES

NOTES

NOTES

CHAPTER 5

A Mother

A mother is a child's first connection in the world. As a child, your mother is the person that you look up to for protection. Your mother is the person that you spend the most important years of your life with. She is the person that you watch and learn most of your traits from. Your mother is your idol at the beginning of your life until you find your own identity. As your child's role model, it is important that we exhibit good behavior and guide our children in the right direction in life. If we are broken and have not found our own identity, we can't teach our children what they need or guide them to find their identity. It would be like the blind leading the blind. If we are clubbing every weekend, fighting, and sleeping around with random men or other people's husbands, you can be sure that our daughters will mimic the behavior that is presented to them. It is extremely hard to rewire a child who has been taught destructive behavior, whether directly or indirectly by their mother. I had a foul mouth and I used to curse around my children. Cursing was my second nature, needless to say, my youngest son picked up the nasty habit at a very early age. He could barely talk but he would curse. It

51

was very embarrassing because he would wait until we were out in public and every other word came out of his mouth when he couldn't have his way or get something he wanted. I would tell him to stop cursing but he would just get louder the more I tried to get him to stop. I would end up spanking him to get him to stop cursing, that was honestly not his fault. It was a habit that he had learned directly from me, his mother. I would feel so guilty after spanking him because he was only doing what he learned from his mother. So, how could I be spanking him when he assumed the behavior was acceptable because he watched me do it.

It is the same with any destructive behavior that our children see and mimic. It is our responsibility to make sure that we are exhibiting good behavior in front of our children. Our children deserve every opportunity that they can get in the future, that does not include early death or jail. We are their mothers, and I cannot emphasize how important our role is in their lives. A woman has the power to make or break her household by the decisions that she makes and her attitude. Let us not be the reason that our children are not successful. I do understand in some cases where you do all that you can to raise your child correctly and they still travel down the wrong road. However, when you know that you have done all that you can to guide them in the right direction, you don't have to feel guilty about the outcome. Once children become adults there is nothing you can do about the decisions they make. But, what I do know is that they are less likely to go astray when they have been taught and guided in the right direction and have been taught the meaning of respect for themselves, as well as others. Our generation lacks respect for anyone including themselves.

Everyone wants to be popular so badly that they will do anything just to be a part of the status quo, sometimes at the expense of their freedom or even their lives. We are losing our kids, and we are the only people who can save them. I remember when I was growing up, certain games and music were not allowed in our house. Today, video games are promoting robbery, prostitution, and worse. Music glorifies murder, drugs and so much more, and this is what we are allowing in our homes. We cannot even get our kids off the phone, long enough to eat dinner and we are ok with this because honestly after a long day at work, you do not really want to talk, you are just trying to relax. We must start making time, even when we are too tired. We need to get more involved in our children's lives because their minds are being corrupted by what society has glammed up as acceptable. As mothers, we must be nosey as my children call it. You have to be, otherwise you will never know what is going on in their lives until it is too late in some cases. I am so tired of hearing about our babies being killed only to realize it was done by another baby. Now that is two lives lost, one to death and one to jail. Things have gotten so bad that schools are now charging the parents of minor children when they participate in a fight at school, they are also made to go to a class. This tells us that even the school system feels that it is the parent's responsibility to control and teach our children the correct behavior that should be exhibited in school. I agree with this approach because everyone knows that you get a person's attention when you start affecting their money. When you start messing with people's money, you get their undivided attention. Mothers today, are too busy trying to live their best lives and neglecting their responsibilities when it comes to their children. Our children are raising themselves and that is why we have so many of them being killed and going to jail because they have no one to teach them differently. I see so many pictures on social media where mothers are posting their sons holding guns and taking pictures with money. This is what we are teaching our babies from little. We are training our sons to hustle the wrong way by glorifying it. We are telling them that this behavior is acceptable and then when tragedy strikes, we are baffled as to how this has happened to us. Look in the mirror, it is what they were taught from little. It is time for us as mothers to wake up and stop thinking that destructive behavior is cute. We live in a world where no one wants to be told about their destructive behavior even if their behavior is leading them down a path that will end up in severe pain, and then when everything explodes, they blame everyone around them except themselves, even though they were warned but they didn't listen. The problem today is that no one takes responsibility for their actions and the outcome due to the decisions that they have made. It is much easier to blame someone else, even when we know that it is our fault. We are in desperate need of mothers to take their place. Be a mother to the child or children that you have given birth to; your life belongs to that child, and every thought that you have should involve that child. Yes, it is not easy to raise a child, but these children deserve our best effort, they didn't ask to come into the world. My mother was thirteen when she had me, she was just a baby herself, she had not even begun to live life and was now a mother. She had no idea how to be a mother. Thank God that she had my grandmother to help her. I was about five years old when my mother took me from my grandmother. My mother was only seventeen at that time and was now raising me and although she didn't have much experience in raising children, she managed to teach the basic things like, respect for myself, respect for my elders, and that you don't talk back to adults when they are addressing you. I was not a perfect child, by no means did I get into my fair share of trouble but even with that I still managed to remember what my mother had taught me about respect. My mother was only thirteen when she had me, but she was able to teach me at an early age about respect. She was able to do that because she was taught by her mother and remembered it and how important it was, so she passed it on even though she was inexperienced in parenting. I am telling this story to say that, it does not matter how old you are, you can be taught the fundamentals of life and respect, being one of the top three in my book because everything else kind of piggybacks off of respect. If you are taught respect as a child, you will not go out killing and robbing people because you understand that it is wrong and a form of disrespect, to take something from someone that they have worked for and something that you didn't earn. When you are taught respect, you will not go out of the house with all your body exposed and you will not allow someone to take nude pictures of you, and you will not send them to other people either. There are cases where children have been taught respect and they still do the opposite. We must teach our children to be leaders and not followers, if not peer pressure will get them. If we teach our children about respect, and the importance of thinking for themselves in time, there would be fewer issues with our children killing, robbing, and being disrespectful to one another and to their elders. Our next generation is fading away at an amazingly fast and steady pace, and we have got to do something to change the course that they are on. Our number one job on this earth is to be a mother when we have children. No one is perfect at the job and most times we figure it out as we go. It is much easier to figure out when we ourselves are not broken. It is hard to admit to someone that we are broken or that we do not have the answers to something, and we are too porous to ask for help because we don't want to feel vulnerable or like we are being judged for not knowing. I know all too well about being proud and not wanting people to feel like you need them. Because when people feel like you need them, you are at their mercy. I have always been one of those people that did not like asking for help even when I was in desperate need of help because I did not want to have it thrown up in my face later. I would go about feeling helpless because of my pride. I had to learn that everyone needs help at some point in their life because we are not meant to do everything alone. If God created us to be alone, he would not have created Eve for Adam. We are meant to help one another when we see each other in need. We must get out of this mentality that we don't want no one in our business or telling us anything. We must stop getting so defensive about everything that someone says because sometimes, people are only trying to help us by pointing out something that we may not know or see that could save us some heartache and pain in the end. It is time for us to pull together as a community and take back our streets by getting our children back in line at home. Sometimes, we do not discipline our children because we want to be friends with them and this is where we go wrong. You cannot party with your children and try to discipline them too; it's not going to work. You can only do one or the other and being their parent is more important. Like my mother used to say, "You may hate me now but when you look back over your life, one day you will thank me." I can say today that she was right. I am glad that I was not allowed to do some of the things that I wanted to do as a child because had I been allowed to do those things, I would be a different person than I am today, even though she is not here for me to tell her. I am glad that she was strong enough to know and do what was best for me and what I needed, and not what I wanted, just to please myself. We must stop trying to be our children's friends and be their mothers, especially when it could make a difference. A parent should not outlive their children, whether by natural causes or through violence. It is time to save our children. There is nothing worse than the feeling of watching your child go to jail for years, while you feel helpless and hopeless because there is nothing that you can do to save your baby because no matter how old they get, they will always be our baby. We do not have to wait for it to get to that point. We can do something right now while we have time. We have the power to change the outcome, by changing the circumstances and getting involved in every area of our children's lives. It is our job to know who our children are spending time together with and the parents of the children they are hanging out with. It is our responsibility to know where our kids are and what they are doing. We are the parents, and it is time that we take the title seriously. We are the boss, we make the rules, and they have to abide by them.

Question to Ponder

What are some of the things you remember about your mother or the person who took care of you?

_____

_____

_____

_____

_____

_____

_____

NOTES

NOTES

NOTES

CHAPTER 6

A Daughter

"Strength and dignity are her clothing, and her position is strong and secure; she rejoices over the future [the latter day or time to come, knowing that she and her family are in readiness for it]."

-Proverbs: 31:25 KJV

Your daughter is a representation of you, her mother. The bond between a mother and her daughter is like no other. You are her best friend, her secret holder, and the shoulder that she cries on when she is hurting. You are the place where she comes for advice and the arms that make her feel safe when her world is falling apart. You are the person that makes her laugh, the person that she looks up to for guidance. You are her role model, the person that she wants to be like when she grows up. Your daughter is your admirer. So, it is important that we are the best role model that we can be. You are watched closely by your daughter as she grows up and what she sees and learns by watching you will shape her future. We want to create

63

strong, independent, courageous women who are not afraid of their own voices and their own thoughts.

We want to create women who are mind-blowing, world-changing, rule-makers, self-motivated, and game-changers. We want to create women whose presence demands respect and attention when they enter a room. Our daughters are our legacy, and we want our legacy to be great. We are women, and we are the voice that will echo through generations by what we instill in our daughters. From birth, it is our job to make sure that our daughters know their self-worth who they are, and what they possess. It is our job to teach, train, and mold our daughters, and impart in them the skills they will need to possess to be a good woman, a mother, and a wife one day. It is an important job that we must take seriously because it is our job to prepare her for the future. If she is not equipped properly, it will reflect on the mother. It is our job to teach our daughter how to cook, which is why we should know how to cook because we cannot give what we don't have. It is time for us to break away from this mentality that we don't need to know how to cook and that a man can cook for himself. Yes, there is nothing wrong with a man helping out around the house with the duties but we don't want to make it his job. I understand that we are professionals and all, but we should still at least know how to cook a meal for our children. I am not saying we should cook every day. I understand that times have changed but so many women today cannot even boil an egg. We need to learn how to cook, and we must take pride in doing so. If we are to be the complete package, then we should be able to cook a hot meal, clean the house, and work. We expect our man to have a job and to provide for his family, so the least that we can do is fulfill our end of the bargain and that includes cooking and cleaning. If we want our daughters to be the best that they can be then we must train, teach, and supply the necessary tools for success. We cannot partially prepare them and send them out into the world and then wonder why they cannot have a fulfilling and devoted relationship that lasts. The same goes for us, we cannot expect to find Mr. Right when we are not Mrs. Right. We must be what we are looking for. We cannot want a hundred percent when we ourselves are only about forty percent. We must also realize ourselves and teach our daughters that perfect does not exist, only Jesus is perfect. We all have flaws, so the best that you can do is decide what is important to you, what you are willing to deal with and what is a deal breaker. I am not talking about accepting being abused, let us get that straight. I am talking more along the lines of if you can deal with him getting toothpaste in the mirror and not cleaning it things like that, just to be clear. If we go looking for perfection, we will end up alone.

We all have flaws, and we must remember that. I believe that if a man holds down a job, he respects you, loves you and your children and he is loyal. He is a keeper. I can deal with the toothpaste; it may get on my nerves, but it is a sacrifice that I am willing to make for all the important things that matter the most. These are the traits that our daughter should be taught. She should know that it does not matter what other people say about you, what matters is what you think of yourself. Our daughter should know that it is ok to be herself and that she should never let anyone tell her that she should change who she is just to fit into some mold that everyone else is in. Our daughter should know that she was created to stand out not fit in. She should set the trend, not follow it. She was born to be a leader. The earlier our daughters are taught these, the less likely they are to allow what other people do affect their decisions for themselves. It is our job to empower our daughters but to do that, we must be empowered; we must know who we are and the power that we possess. It is time for us to tap into the power that we have inside of us and stop waiting on someone to validate who we are, we do not need validation from anyone other than ourselves. It is our job to look in the mirror and see how beautiful we are. We must motivate ourselves; we have to believe in ourselves, we have to know that we are worth it and that we can do anything that we put our minds to with the strength from God. We are great women, we are beautiful and unique, and it is time that we take our place. It is time we teach our daughters to take their place. It is time we teach our daughters that they are more than their bodies and that you do not have to be half-naked to feel worthy of attention. It is time that we change the message that society has sent, that you must expose yourself if you want to be noticed.

We live in a time that supports women demoralizing themselves to get attention and to succeed. It is time that we take a stand and let everyone know that we are more than our bodies. We have other attributes to offer. It is time that we let our voices be heard, it is demeaning, and we have to change the cycle for our daughters who are coming behind us. The message out there is that if you do not have a small waist, big boobs, and a big butt you cannot succeed and that is not the message that we should be sending. We want our daughters to know that they are beautiful regardless of their size, hair, or skin color. You are perfect just the way that you are. Embrace who you are and know that you are lacking nothing. Everything you need is already in you, dream big and never let anyone tell you that you cannot accomplish whatever you put your mind to. You were created to soar like an eagle, to live the best life that you can dream. Every young girl wants to hear that they are beautiful, that they are smart, that they can do anything. It is our job as mothers to build our daughter's self-esteem, so we have to be very careful of how we talk to our daughters as well as what we call our daughters. When you call them names like whore, bitch, etc, that is what they will be. If someone in the streets or a man addresses them that way, they will feel that it is ok because that is what they are called at home by their own mother. If we tell our daughters that they are dumb and will never amount to anything, they will go through life believing it because that is what they have been programmed to believe, and if your mother is the one telling it to you, that one person who is supposed to love and protect you, why would you not believe her. If we are the ones tearing our daughters down instead of building up their self-esteem then how do we expect them to believe that they can do anything other than to fail? How can you expect them to demand respect from someone else when they are not respected by their own mother? It is our job to build our daughters up.

She is a precious gift from God that needs nurturing and all the love that a mother can give. there is nothing like the love of a mother. It makes a child feel safe, important, and wanted. They can't buy that feeling. A child looks for approval from their parents, they need lots of attention and if they are not getting it, they will do everything possible to get the attention. So, it is important that when we see negative behavior, we get to the root of the problem before we can assume the worst. Our children say that they love the attention and if you are not in their business, they wouldn't feel like you care. If we think back to when we ourselves were children, I know I used to say I hated my mother being all in my business but if she didn't ask me how my day was, I felt as if something was wrong. It is particularly important to have dialogues with your children, especially your daughters. It is how they know that they can talk to you and build a bond of strong and lasting relationship. I told my mother everything and I mean everything. Sometimes she would tell me it was too much information; she was my best friend as I got older. As women, we look for friendships and relationships where we can be ourselves and be accepted and somewhere along the line, our radar gets off track because we meet people who then try to change us into the person that they feel we should be, and before it is over. We have allowed so many people to come in and out of our lives and change a piece of us or take a piece of us that now we have lost the very essence of being who we were before they came along. We begin to doubt ourselves and our worth. We began to think that something is wrong with us and that is just not the truth.

It took me a long time to realize that I shouldn't have to change who I am to be accepted. True acceptance is allowing yourself to be your complete and honest self, and a true friend or partner accepts all of you and they don't try to change you. If someone leaves, let them leave, why try to persuade someone to stay in your life when they no longer want to be there? It is truly their loss, not yours. I look back at how long it took me to realize this, I spent so many years trying to be what other people wanted me to be in relationships and I also look back and realize that even in the midst of trying to be what my partner wanted, it still didn't last, and now I understand because it was not real and I was not being me. You cannot pretend to be someone else for so long. Eventually, you get tired, and you begin to resent the other person. You will never be able to have a meaningful and loving relationship with anyone unless it is built on complete honesty and that means being yourself. If someone loves you, they want you to be you and they do not try to change you. I look at my daughters right now and I see some of the same traits that I possess in them and their relationships and this is why I say that the cycle must be broken, it must stop with me. No one should have to compromise their beliefs to satisfy someone else, you should not have to change or dumb yourself down to please a man so that his ego is not bruised. It is not our responsibility to coddle him, he is a man. I look at what is going on right now with our children and it saddens me because they deserve so much more, and we are obligated to make sure that they have everything that they need to survive in this brutal and dying world. We are their mothers, if we do not do it, it will not get done. We are their only hope for survival and it is particularly important that we understand this. If our children are not equipped properly with the tools that they need for survival, it is our fault when they fail because we did not do our job as mothers. Everyone says that a man runs the house, but I honestly disagree with that, and here is why. Yes, a real man works and he takes care of the financial portion of the home and he steps in to discipline the children when it is truly needed. A real woman/mother takes care of the home, she makes sure that the bills get paid when the money comes in. She is the one who spends all the time with the children, raising them by guiding and teaching them the right things to do. She is the person that keeps the family together. So, it is very important that the woman knows her role and takes that role seriously because her family depends on her for guidance, and without that guidance, the family could be doomed. Rise, women, arise and take your place.

Question to Ponder

As a daughter, what are some of the things that you remember growing up that have shaped you as a person?

_____

_____

_____

_____

_____

_____

_____

NOTES

NOTES

NOTES

CHAPTER 7

A Sister

God is in the midst of her, she shall not be moved; God will help her right early [at the dawn of the morning].

-Psalms: 46:5 KJV

As a child, your sister is the second person that you should love besides your mother. As you get older and begin to venture off, your sister will become your secret keeper, the person that you tell what you do not want your mother to know. Your sister will know things about you that your mother will never know. She is that person that you will talk to when you feel there is no one else in the world that you can talk to. She is that person who will not judge you no matter how bad it may be or sound. She is the one person you can depend on to keep your dirty secrets. My sister was that person who literally took a whipping for me because she wouldn't tell on me. She would open the door for me whenever I snuck out of the house. She would even lie and say that she did things that we both knew I had done alone and even when she was getting whipped, she still would never tell on me. When you are growing up and trying to find your way, your sister is the person who always has your back. If you are an older sister, your little sister is watching you closely and will mimic everything that you do because she wants to be just like you. It is important that you, as an older sister set good examples for your little sister. Teach her to be independent and not to follow others just for the sake of being down.

When your mother is not there or present, your sister by default becomes the person that you look to for guidance. She becomes that person that you look to for guidance and protection. She is your safety blanket. Your sister is the person who runs away with you because she does not want you out there alone. Your sister is the person who sits back-to-back with you while taking turns to sleep in an abandoned house because you have nowhere else to go. Your sister is the person who goes to jail with you because you broke into your own house and your parents sent you to jail. Your sister is the person who is going to be there for you, your entire life whether you are right or wrong. She is your true ride or die. She is your friend, in some cases, she takes the place of your mother and she bares your pains and brokenness. I thank God for my sister because if he hadn't sent her, I would've had to endure all those terrible moments alone. It is so much easier when you are finding your way and you not to be alone. It feels so much better when you have someone to share those horrible times with. Someone who you can trust. Someone that one day when it has all come to pass you can sit down, laugh, and cry if need be about all the things that you have survived together.

Life is nothing more than a journey and the outcome depends on how we go through that journey, and what we learn from the journey. I believe that a sister is an angel sent down from God to help guide you through the tough times that you are sure to endure in this life. He knew what you have to go through, so he sent you someone that you could confide in. Someone that you could completely be your true self with. He sent you someone who is there to hold your hand in your darkest times and tell you that it is going to be ok and that you are going to make it. Your sister is someone who will hold your hand and pull you through when you don't have an ounce of strength left to go on. Your sister is the person who tells you that joke that makes you cry and laugh even when you are at your worst and your eyes are swollen from crying all night from that broken heart. Your sister is your living diary, the place where you put all your deepest thoughts, all your dreams, all your pain and betrayals in this life. Your sister is the person that knows you like no one else in the world will ever really know you because half of the stuff that the two of you have done and the secrets that you know will never be repeated to a living soul, it will go to the graves with you. A sister is a gift from God, sent to earth to make the load that you will have to carry just a little lighter, knowing that you have someone that you can share the weight of life with. There will be times when you will not see each other eye to eye, but those times will be overcome by the unbreakable bond that you share. No one in life will know you better than a sibling who has grew up in the same house with you, the person who has seen you at your very worst and at your absolute best. The person who deep down inside wonders exactly how the two of you survived all that you have survived together. The reason you have survived is because you had each other. While you were growing up, your sister was there at every turn for the good and especially the bad. When you cried she cried, when you laughed she laughed, when you fought she fought, it didn't matter if you were wrong, she was right there beside you through it all. Your sister is one of the things that will always be constant in your life. You do not have to worry about her leaving you, no matter where you go or what happens, you will always be bound to one another. You are one another's keeper. Whenever you call on your sister, she will always come running, no matter where you are or what time of the day or night it is, she is only a phone call away.

Question to Ponder

What are some of the secrets that you remember telling your sister, or the person that you considered to be like a sister?

_____

_____

_____

_____

_____

_____

_____

NOTES

NOTES

NOTES

CHAPTER 8

I Am

But by the grace of God, I am what I am, and his grace toward me was not for nothing. In fact, I worked harder than all of them, though it was not really, I, but the grace of God which was with me.)

-1 Corinthians: 15:10 KJV

On June 18, 1977, a little Black girl named Christena Marie Rollins was born to Freddie Mae Rollins. Because Freddie Mae Rollins was only thirteen when she gave birth, her mother took on the responsibility of raising little Christena. I, Christena, returned back to my mother, Freddie Mae, who was now about eighteen. My mother was living with my stepdad who later adopted me. My stepdad was not the easiest person to get along with, I feared him and didn't like him, and he didn't really like me much either. He was a drunk who did not know how to manage his liquor. He would come home drunk, fuss with my mother, and break things in the house. It was scary in the house as a child. When I was about eleven, I remember him fighting with my mother and I yelled at him for fighting with my mother and I told him to stop hitting her. He struck me and told me to shut up. After this situation, I knew he really didn't like me and had it out for me for sure and I knew it. I hated living in that house, it was not a home at all. We were not to go outside, he would always ground us for no reason. We were not allowed to play with the other kids in the neighborhood because he was afraid that we would tell someone what was really going on in our house, and it would tarnish his reputation as a nice, friendly, and helpful neighbor. I always felt that he was two different personalities, the nice person to all the people in the streets and in the neighborhood and then the old, evil person that we got to see behind closed doors. When I was about thirteen, I remember my mother being hurt on her job and she had to have surgery.

When she had the surgery at the hospital, she got a staph infection in her back and she couldn't walk for almost a year. She was in the hospital for about four months before she came home. So, we were there with him alone. I will never forget that feeling of complete helplessness. I wanted to stay at the hospital with my mother. I did not feel safe being alone with him. I did not trust him at all. I remember him telling me that he did not trust me at all. I remember him telling me that he didn't like me because I had the same name as his sister whom he hates so much because his dad loved her and her mother more. His dad had her from cheating on his mother so I was a reminder of that pain in his life because of my name. He said that no one he ever knew that was named Christena was good or amounted to anything. He said I was not going to amount to anything because of my name. I remember how that made me feel but I also remember telling my sister that I wished he would just drop dead. I did not trust him or like him and when I was about fourteen, I found out why. I have never told anyone this, not my mother who is now deceased, not my sister whom I tell everything. No one, I have carried this inside of me for so long that right now I am shaking and can barely breathe. I will never forget the horrible feeling. I was in the bathroom on the toilet, and he knocked on the bathroom door and asked for some tissue. I opened the bathroom door and went to hand him the tissue, but he came in and closed the door. He began to touch me, he put his hands in my panties and touched me. I asked him what he was doing, and he just looked at me and never said a word. I was so angry with myself, and I felt so dirty that I did not do anything other than say what are you doing. I just kept trying to figure out how I would tell my mother what had happened. Would she believe me if he made up some lie and then stuck it to me? I felt so helpless. My mother could not walk and telling her wouldn't change anything. She won't be able to do anything about it, so I never told a soul. I locked it away inside and tried my best to forget that it happened. A few weeks later he attempted to touch me again but this time I bit him and told him that if he touched me again, I was going to call the police on him. I never told anyone because I was embarrassed and ashamed that something like this could happen to me. I felt that if I told someone, that meant it really happened in my mind. I felt that if I never talked about it, then it never happened. I know that I am not the only one with a story like this and what I did not know was that by not telling anyone that this happened to me, I allowed the pain to take me captive and I never healed from it, nor did I ever forgive him for what he did. He has been dead for well over eighteen years and he still had a hold on me because of what he had done to me as a child. I never realized that until I submitted my life to God and began to read the bible. I began to remember things from my childhood that I did not want to remember, that being one of them. I had done a really good job of burying it to the point that I had really made myself believe that it had never happened, but it did, and I needed to face it and let it go. I had to be healed and to do that I had to admit to myself that it had happened and release it.

When I was fifteen, I went to court and begged the judge to put me in a group home. I remember the judge asking my mom what was going on at the house that I would rather be in a group than there. I remember my mother crying because I did not want to be at home with her, it broke my heart, but I just couldn't be there in that house with him anymore, I had to get out. My mother asked me what was wrong and everything in me wanted to be honest with her but all I could think of was, what if she didn't believe me, or what if she did believe me but didn't leave him? Our relationship would never be the same, I would rather not know because I loved my mother but she wasn't always the strongest woman that I knew when it came to him. I went to a group home and lived there until I was eighteen at that point, I could no longer live there. I was released with nowhere to go, so I went back home. I thought for some strange reason, that things might be a little better because I was older now and I was not afraid to speak my mind. I was so wrong, he was still controlling and mean as always. I got a job at a hotel downtown and when I got my first check, he wanted the whole check. I offered half of the check but he demanded the whole check, I refused and was put out. It was eight at night, I had nowhere to go, but I had a nine hundred dollar check.

I called the only person I could think of and that was one of the house mothers from the group home that I lived in, we had become close while I was there. She took me in and let me stay with her and her husband, I paid her four hundred dollars a month to stay there but I had my own room, freedom, and a key. I felt safe and that was priceless. I thought I was safe until things changed. In the beginning, everything was going well. I would go to work and come home anytime, I didn't have a curfew, but I always tried to be in by midnight to show respect unless I was sleeping out. Everything was going well and I called her my aunt because that is what she was like to me. My aunt worked two jobs, but her husband didn't work at all, so she worked a lot and overnight a lot. I had no problems because she was barely there and her husband was always running the streets at least in the beginning until one day I was off, and I was at the house sitting in the living room watching television when he came home. He walked in the door and said hello, I spoke and then he went into his room. He left a few minutes later. He said that he wanted to talk to me about something. I thought that I had done something wrong but instead, he began to tell me that the husband of our neighbor upstairs asked him how it felt to be sleeping with two women living under the same roof. My stomach began to cringe because here I was and it was happening all over again. He forced himself on me even though I asked him not to, I remember him saying oh stop acting like you are a virgin. You have a boyfriend and I know you do fuck him. I just began to cry because I could not believe that this was happening again. I told him that I was going to tell my aunt and he started choking me and said that I was not going to tell her anything because he would kill me first. I was so scared, I didn't know what to do. All I could think of was what he said he would do to me and I wondered if I told her would she even believe me. So, I stayed quiet and didn't report to my aunt.

For two months, he would wait until she was at work and come back to the house and make me have sex with him. I know that most people would wonder why I stayed and let him continue to have sex with me. It is easy for someone outside looking in to pass judgement when they themselves have never been through something like this. Fear literally paralyzes you. When I think about it as I write this, there were different reasons that I stayed and number one is, honestly because I had nowhere to go, I would've been on the streets, and as he said, it wasn't like I was a virgin and I was terrified of him. I was eighteen with nowhere to go, so even though I did not want to have sex with him, I had a roof over my head and food to eat. In life, people will use your circumstances to take advantage of you in the worst way. He knew that I had nowhere to go, so he took advantage of me. He knew that I was afraid of being on the street, so he used it to his advantage. I eventually moved out and never spoke to my aunt again who I felt was also taking advantage of me, I was paying her four hundred dollars a month to stay with her. She was also making me give her a hundred and fifty dollars that she said she was saving for me so I could get my own place, well, needless to say. when I left, I never got a dime of the money that she said she was saving, so she kept all of my money. You trust people and they take advantage of you. The very same people who say that they are only trying to help are some of the main people who mistreat you and take advantage of you for whatever they get out of you. I had no place to go, so I went to the Covenant House where I lived for a couple of months until I had my first son, then I moved in with his dad. Life has truly been a journey of ups and downs, I have been mistreated, taken advantage of, beaten, and abused mentally, physically, and emotionally. I have been talked down on, lied to, and I have been used and through it all, I, Christena Marie Rollins, am still standing. I am a survivor!

Question to Ponder

Who are you in your own eyes?

_____

_____

_____

_____

_____

_____

_____

NOTES

NOTES

NOTES

CHAPTER 9

We Are

I will praise thee; for I am fearfully and wonderfully made:
marvelous are thy works; and that my soul knoweth right well.

-Psalms 139: 14 KJV

In life, we have all been hurt, we have all suffered some type of pain and betrayal and because of that pain, pieces of us have been chipped away. We are broken to some degree, but the good news is that we can be healed and set free from the things that have held us captive in our past. We have got to understand that everything that we've been through in life has caused us pain, there was a lesson attached to learn and it has shaped us and formed us into who we have become today. In life, we will have to go through these difficult moments, but we have to understand that they are to strengthen us and push us to the next level in life. Everything that we go through in life, can help someone else one day that may be going through the very thing that we had been through and survived. No one wants to be hurt or to feel pain but if through your pain which you have survived, someone else is motivated and has the hope that they can survive theirs, then what you went through was not in vain.

We are all connected to some degree through our pain. We have all experienced some of the same type of pain or heartache in our lives. If we know how it feels to have our hearts broken, why would we want to be a part of the process that causes the pain in the first place? Why would we want to cause that kind of pain to another person? We live in a world that believes it is ok to do hurtful things to other people, but we do not want those very things done to us. If we started to think about our actions and the pain that our actions would cause, I think we would be less likely to do things that will cause pain to others. It is easy to do mean and hurtful things to other people without giving it a second thought, until the very thing that we have done to someone else is done to us, only then, do we understand because we are the ones feeling the pain from the action and on the receiving end. Who we are today, is a direct reflection of the things that we have been through in life. Everyone has their own story and no matter what that story is, we all have the power to overcome it. God says, "All things work together for the good of those that love the Lord; that are called according to his purpose." It does not matter what it is that you have been through, God will use it and turn it around for your good. We all have something that we are insecure about, that no one knows about but us because it is our little secret.

We have all been hurt, betrayed, and lied to at some point in our lives, and yet we are still standing, we are all still alive fighting to survive in a world that has grown so cold and numb toward one another. We have become so focused on ourselves and what we want that we are willing to tear each other down and ruin one another. We should be helping one another and lifting one another up because that is what God wants us to do. Love one another as we love ourselves. We are so scared that we will not make it or that someone else will get there before us, so we do everything in our power to make sure that no one gets there before us. Once we are there, if anyone else comes along and we feel threatened by their existence, then we do everything in our power to make sure that we destroy that person and make them look bad, all because we are insecure. Insecurities come from a place deep down inside you, feelings of unbelief in yourself. You feel less than capable. If you believe in yourself and know that you are doing your best you have no reason to feel inferior to anyone else. We are not in competition with anyone, so there is no need to compare yourself to anyone else. We have to stay in our own lane and focus on being the very best at doing what we are good at and nothing else will matter. We have to first find out what we are good at as an individual and stick with that, perfect that thing and be the best at it.

We are all good at something and have something to offer the world that only we can give. We just must figure out what that thing is. We go through life and sometimes we get lost and forget who we are as life and the struggles and pains of life strip us of pieces of our being, somewhere along the way we get caught up in the waves and begin to take on the form of the struggles and the pain that has attached itself to us in place of what it stripped away. Our confidence, our trust in other people, our love for people and life. When this happens, we begin to see life differently. We get to a place where we feel that everyone in the world around us is out to get us and take something from us, and we begin to believe that the only way that we can survive is to get them before they get us. The rape we had to endure taught us that no one can be trusted. When our mothers didn't love us the way she should, that taught us that if she didn't love us, something had to be wrong with us. When the friend that you trusted with all your secrets betrayed you, it taught us everyone is fake. Life has a way of beating you down and stripping the best parts of who you are away if you let it. It is important that we meet the people who have come into our lives and do not value us. We must remember that there are good and genuine people in the world. If we allow the people who have hurt us to rob us of living and let other people into our lives, we will never know what it is like to truly bond with others and form stable relationships. There will always be those people who go through life, preying on others and wreaking havoc.

We just have to get to a place where we pay attention to the red flags when we see them and eventually, we will see them coming because they are all the same and carry the same traits. We must get to a place in life where we don't allow the bad things that have happened to keep us from loving, and trusting because, without those two things, we can never truly be happy. No one knows what tomorrow holds, so we have to take advantage of every day that we are blessed to have and enjoy life and live it to the fullest. We can't allow bad people to make us afraid and think that just because they are bad, everyone we meet will be the same way. We must judge people according to their own actions and not the actions of someone before them. We are all responsible for our own actions and on judgment day we will have to answer for those actions. We cannot allow the actions of other people to change who we are and make us just as they are because we have been hurt, if we become like them, we are no better than them. We can't allow the pain that others have inflicted on us to cause us to hurt others, we have to find a way to love no matter what has happened in our lives, or the world will be without love, We have got to change the cycle and someone has to be bold enough to step out with faith and be the change we all want to see. If no one ever takes the step to make the change, we will all be doomed and the cycle will continue to repeat itself through our children. I don't want my children to miss out on love and feeling true happiness, we all deserve love and true happiness and it does exist. We have to show love even when we ourselves have not been shown love.

We have all been lied to, we have all been heartbroken, we have all been betrayed by someone we thought we could trust and even though the pain of it all was almost unbearable, you made it and it made you stronger and wiser. In life, we must take the lessons that we have been taught and apply them to our everyday lives. If we've experienced hurt and understand its impact, realizing it's not a feeling we'd wish to endure repeatedly, we shouldn't desire to burden our conscience by inflicting similar pains on others, if we inflict that kind of pain on another person then we are no better than the very people who have caused us the same pain.

We were created to love and help one another when in need, we were never meant to compete with one another or tear each other down with mean and hateful words or deeds. When we feel the need to hurt others, we should stop and really evaluate what the root of the problem really is and try to resolve it within ourselves. When you feel the need to inflict harm on someone else, it is something deep down in yourself that needs healing. If we begin to deal with what the real issues are of our insecurities, we will find that most of the things that we think are a problem are really things that we have made up in our own mind due to pain from our past or our experiences with other people that have left us broken to some extent, when we make peace with the things of our past and forgive those who have wronged us even when they do not apologize. We will be able to move on and truly heal and not hold other people responsible for something that was done by someone before them.

Life can sometimes get the best of us and the pain that we feel along with the unforgiveness that we are holding on to, can take us captive and cause us to believe things that are not completely true about others. We must free ourselves of that baggage that we have been carrying from past hurts. We have got to get rid of the baggage because it is weighing us down and causing us to be unable to look up and see a better day and a better way of living. Tomorrow is not promised in life, so why waste one day focused on the past; we cannot move toward the future if we are stuck in the past. We are all connected in some way through our pain, let us not get stuck in the past and miss our beautiful future. We are all survivors of something, now, it is time to live! And let go of the past, the future is waiting, and it looks so promising.

Question to Ponder

What do you believe that we can do to bring unity?

_____

_____

_____

_____

_____

_____

_____

_____

NOTES

NOTES

NOTES

CHAPTER 10

The Trauma

Some things have happened in our lives, starting from our childhood that have shaped some of our lives and have altered the way we think, see things, and function. Some things are so painful that we don't even want to think about them or discuss them because we would rather forget they ever happened. The bad thing about not talking about it is that, we won't get the healing we need, and because we never faced and confronted the trauma, it takes us prisoner. when we become prisoners to the very thing that we are hiding from, it starts to change our very existence.

Trauma causes us to distrust, and to question everything. Trauma causes us to become bitter, angry, and unhappy beings in some cases. We are angry with everyone that we come in contact with in some cases. We start to think that everyone is out to get us and take something from us. Trauma that is not confronted robs us of our joy, peace, and happiness, it robs us of genuine relationships in some cases. When we don't deal with our past trauma and then start to have children, we teach our children from a place of pain, which means what they are learning is distorted. For example: a mother who may have been sexually abused as a child doesn't trust anyone. Therefore, she questions all male relationships and because she assumes that she is protecting her child or children, she doesn't let them out of her sight, she doesn't allow them to go anywhere that causes them to be away from her, in her mind, she's doing what a mother should do to protect her kids. Not realizing that she is keeping her children from enjoying their childhood, which in some cases the overbearing protection puts a strain on the relationship with your children, especially since your children do not understand the behavior because you do not talk about your trauma with anyone. When we do not get healed from our past trauma, it affects the decisions that we make and therefore can in some cases destroy relationships because of our inability to trust or see good in others. It is very important to get help by talking about and releasing the things that we have been through in our past so that we don't take them into our future.

When we allow trauma to fester and we don't talk about it, we make irrational decisions from a place of pain and hurt, sometimes even anger and bitterness because our view has been distorted by the things that we have been through. When we bring children into the situation because we are instructing and teaching from a place of hidden hurt and pain, we sometimes hurt our children and also their future as well. If for no other reason, that is why we must seek help to navigate through the trauma that has caused us pain.

Unresolved trauma does not just affect us, it affects our children and it affects everyone that we come in contact with in our lives. In order to make sure that our relationships are positive and built on a solid foundation, it is important for us to make sure that we get the help we need by talking to someone who can help us navigate through the trauma and the pain. We must also understand that there is no reason for us to feel guilty about the things that we have gone through in life that have caused so much trauma and love scars that it is not our fault, so therefore, there is no reason for us to feel ashamed of the things that we have been through in life. There is no need to hide anymore, it is time for us to understand that we were the victims, we are not to be blamed for the bad things that have happened in our lives especially, as children, We don't talk about the things that we've been through because we are too ashamed, and we don't want people to look at us as damaged goods. It is okay to get help, it is not our fault and if for nothing else, we should do it for our children so that they do not become products of our trauma.

Question to Ponder

How have you to this point processed the trauma from your childhood and now?

_____

_____

_____

_____

_____

_____

NOTES

NOTES

NOTES

_____

_____

_____

_____

_____

_____

_____

_____

CHAPTER 11

The Release

Today, as I come to the end of this book, I ask that we all take an inventory of our lives and lay to rest everything that needs to be buried, so that we may move forward. I vow to live a life full of joy and true happiness, I will love hard, and I will trust again unless I am given a reason not to. I will judge everyone according to their own deeds and not from anything or anyone from my past. We are all individual people and should be treated as such. I will smile more and laugh more. I will explore unknown territories; I will allow the rain to fall on my face. I will focus on what is ahead of me and not behind me. Today, I lay my past to rest, and I will never look back at it again. Today, I only look forward to what is in front of me and what is to come. I will accept that everything that has happened in my life has brought me to the very place that I am in right now and know that even in pain there was good. It made me stronger, and wiser and it gave me the determination to survive like never before and for that, I will forever be grateful. I forgive everyone that has ever hurt me, I forgive every one that did not believe in me and talked about me behind my back. I also pray that anyone that I may have hurt throughout my journey to finding myself will forgive me.

I truly apologize, my intentions were never to hurt anyone. I am not where God wanted me to be, but I have grown, and I am not the person that I was yesterday. I look forward to becoming the woman that God created me to be, I look forward to fulfilling the purpose that I was destined for before I was born. I am anticipating meeting the woman that I was born to be and while on the journey to become her, I will make mistakes, I know that I will fall sometimes but I promise to get up and dust myself off and to never stay down too long. Life is a journey full of ups and downs, and heartache but there is a lesson in every pain. Don't focus so much on the downs that you miss the ups or the good people that come into your life and pour into it even if they don't stay forever.

Do not forget to enjoy the good times on the journey because those are the moments that count the most and those are the times that kept you as well. If you only remember the downs, you risk being bitter and mad at the world and begin to believe that no good exists, so we must remember the good because it helps us to balance out the good and the bad. We must remember that there are good people in the world and that all hope is not lost. It is time that we choose life, it is time that we choose to live a life that is full of joy and happiness, we only get one chance at living so why waste it on people who never deserved us in the first place? It is not our fault that the people who hurt us or walked out of our lives left. They were broken themselves and we're hurting and they were lost so we have to forgive them and let them go in order to step into our future. We must leave all the heavy baggage behind; it is time for us to embrace what is before us, it is time for us to live a life of joy and peace. I say goodbye to the little girl, I release her, and I say hello to the woman that I am right now and to the woman I have yet to become. God has sounded the alarm and it is time to wake up. Women of God, you are needed, it is time to take your place.

Question to Ponder

What are the things that you need to release to move forward?

_____

_____

_____

_____

_____

_____

_____

NOTES

NOTES

NOTES

A LETTER TO THE LITTLE GIRL

The day that you were born, heaven in their system admired the beautiful and wonderful work of God. Heaven knew that Earth had been blessed with an angel. An incredibly unique and special Angel created to do a job and fulfill a destiny that only you can do. You were created with a purpose. You are one of a kind. There is no one like you, no one else can fit the mold, they are not supposed to. Your head is shaped exactly as I designed it to be, your eyes were placed in the very position that they were meant to be, your nose, your smile, your ears, the length of your arms, your fingers, your legs, your skin color, your feet, the toes on your feet down to the shape of your body and every strand of hair on your head whether it be long, short, straight or curly.

I took my time, and every detail of your being was well thought out and done in love. You look exactly as you were created to look; you are beautiful, wonderful, and one-of-a-kind. I love you for your authenticity, I love you for your compassionate and caring nature. I love you for you and every single part of you. Embrace your uniqueness. It is what sets you apart from everyone else It is what makes you smile. I took my time with you; you are perfect in every way, and it is time for you to do what you were created to do. Shine as only you can do and take your place. The world has been waiting for you. Make your mark and remember that I am always with you, no matter where you go. I am only a call away. Love always, your father, your creator, your way maker, your deliverer, your friend in a time of me.

You are ready, and you can do it, believe in yourself as I believe in you.

The End

www.ingramcontent.com/pod-product-compliance
Lightning Source LLC
Chambersburg PA
CBHW060325130626
46553CB00003B/916